Time & Knots

Dear Gurspreet,

Wishing you the Best!

Gaganjit Singh

Time & Knots

Taran Singh

ISBN 13: 9781729254547

Contents

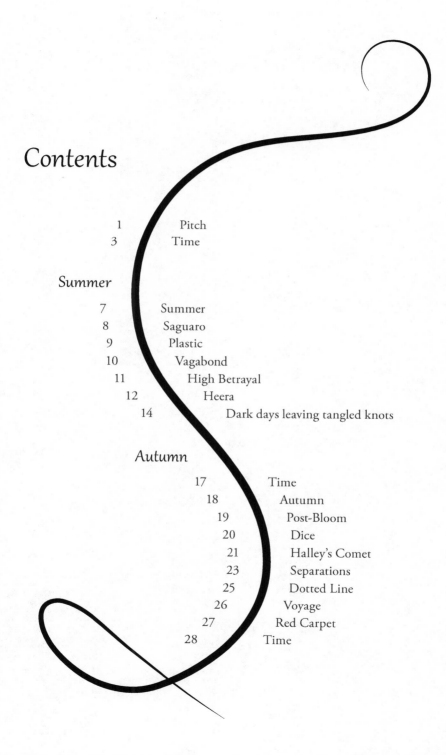

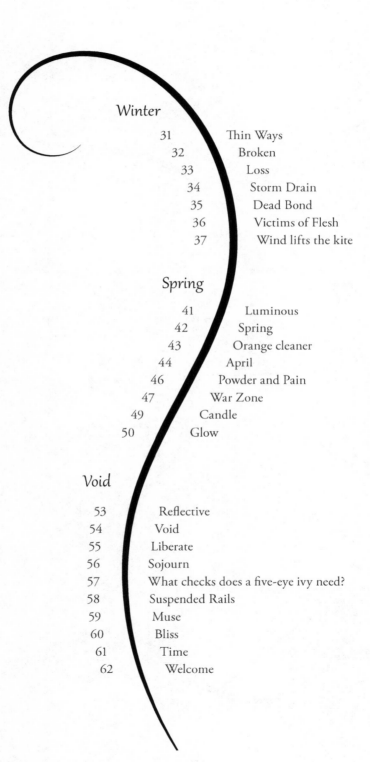

Dear reader,

Time is a mesmerizing ocean in its whirlpool of now, before,
and after - we explore, discover, and anchor onto threads
that shape our destiny, ethos, and footprints. Time & Knots is
a humble effort to put this kaleidoscope of us in a poetic expression.

I crafted this book in time's cyclical pattern with each poem
and section intermingled in the cosmic sea of seasons.
The poems are progressive but still hold their individual shore;
they are like crests and troughs carrying forward the ink.
Within those movements, there is abundant sprinkle of pause
and space for you to enjoy this collection through exhale and inhale.

I've also taken the opportunity to annotate each section
of this collection in gurmukhi script, an honor to the language
and medium that has fostered and fueled this journey.

I welcome you to explore this voyage and enjoy the unfurling
of Time & Knots.

Taran

Time & Knots

ਵੇਲਾ ਤੇ ਗੰਢਾਂ

ਤਰਨ ਜੀਤ ਸਿੰਘ

Pitch

The first page is blank.

Like the pure soul,
the cosmic expanse needs no ink.
The title is short with an and,
to connect the rhythm with nodes.

Index a dubious clock
with winding ticks,
knocking beats,
relieving beliefs,
runny feet,
healing wheel,

The journey resets and repeats.

Inside the fine print: a spirit folding and unfolding

tales of human's knots
screaming in voids
resilient streams
the ethereal shine
the lofty might
broken pulls and salient strings
dusk shadows and love pouring.

Seeds are longing and peace burgeoning—
the journey that resets and repeats.

T. Singh

Time

oscillating away in seasonal currents
tugging strong on every pulse.
Time, striking on its silent wings
moments of grief, guilt, joy and bliss.
In dawn and dusk
reiterating the eminent universal hymn
in heart, mind and soul.

Time...
ceaselessly stirring parallel worlds

T. Singh

ਹੁਨਾਲ਼

Summer

T. Singh

Summer

Summer has gone
along with the plays—
exotic birds trapped in a staged world.

Ironic colorful plumages—
liberating melodies and boastful flights.
They cast a long shadow.

By design, distractions ensure
we are prisoners
with love for civilized lust.
Gullible legs are trapped
by the allure of open sky—
> *Our deep fondness robbed.*
> *Our nurturing unison breached.*
> *Our sacred footprints obliterated.*

Crestfallen and bound to wire frames—
> *Our lives shrink beyond scale.*
> *Our melodies distressed, wings clipped.*
> *Our hearts pierced and moments seized.*

—love birds cleaved by a callous world.

Saguaro

In the heat of growth a million thorns throng our flesh.
Though our visage high, and our view expansive,
we are lowly.

Torrid winds have scorched us.
Thirsty from endless desire, we find no relief.
Signs sear us from the unknown.
The Gila woodpecker hollows out our spines.
An opening preserves new life.

Shaken—a bit hollow—
and attuned to the *chreeps* of fledglings,
we learn to extend our arms
knowing we can bear the burning pain,
for the embrace of fleeting holds.

Plastic

Our burden, heavy
on thorny buds,
loose stalks high
on artificial red.

There's a hole between us
that plucks pleasure
and muzzles shiny matter.

We are animals of want.
Our ante of love is cheap.

Real me died years ago.
Still, bury me with a garland
of scarlet skulls.

Vagabond

Dazzling days diminish;
blind nights remain. They grow
darker in hollow stakes.

Such contrast conceals our kismet—
     destiny's breath unleashed.

A slow learner,
     I wander the
rolling hills.

In the quivering,
     my heart, enticed,
sprints through the dark,
oblivious to disappearing acts of the moon.

A paradise is lost
to gain a sky of sighs.

 A slow healer,
     I reel
from love-inflicted wounds.

Discovered boundaries
     first claim, then chain.

T. Singh

High Betrayal

Holds are tight on the sharp ledge.
Ascent with hammered pins
and hardened grips.
Death hovers close
on perilous granite cliffs.

Follow this strange world
through its cracked course
where a kiss seals truthfulness
and bares hollowness.

Glacier-scarred chins
are only scalable by internal flaws.
The cracks are hidden on
precipice and heart—
we cling with fearless trust.

High roof our trusted abode
we rock—steady in ascent and descent.
Our climbs become songs and, all along,
you cunningly hide an unscalable face.

A knot is undone.
Warm grip, cold and pinless
the defining threads
—a voiding hold.

Heera

Four parts sand, one sack of cement densely packed—
and countless stones crushed and
staged like weathered ridges around a pool.

Heera, my mother, is adorned in prismatic
charm—morning shine. Spirit tall, her stance reigns
higher than columns of pines. Her illuminating hands seize the
rusty shovel, eager to unsettle time's breeze.

She moves surely—a reckoning titanium force.
There is no straw of hesitation in her daily burdens.
The half-hopeless man is passed out on the bed;
she breaks dawn's silence with whispers to divine
proffering sugary chai—her sweetness boundless
in her milk, a nourishing thunder.

While the crackling rays flit around peaks,
she wraps me in warmth,
trekking to work with a humbling pride.
Somewhere in her rhythm and humming is our passage.

At work, the cross-section of sand and stone,
she daily toils beyond any measurable ruler or clock.
Before her industry and sweat, she secures me,
neatly looping a circumference of knotted rope around my waist
—the other end steadily held.

My day's muses are noticeable shapes—
crushed stones, flakes of pine cones,
my untethered imagination flowing on the sandy floor.
Heera keeps me mesmerized with her mountain spirit,
her enduring mold, always the mortar of my core.

Four parts day, one sky packed with stars,
and countless pearls stacked high around a pool.
She delicately brushes the day away and lifts me in her shine,
swirling and singing to me
like heaven musing to contented time.

Dark days leaving tangled knots

 endless frictionless moments,
unsaid words bundling hours,
low tides that drown the visible upside—
I'm just another wayside.

I belong to the invincible
committed to live in pride!

Chilling nightmares swallowing full moons,
trusted backs betrayed in plain sight,
countless treasons exploding into desires,
heartless wounds from friendly fires—
I succumb and cede.

I belong to the invictus
destined to succeed!

Hardened bites gnashing to defeat,
fleeing feet with perfectly timed retreats,
painted windows entreated then ignored,
locked doors proclaiming no more strangers aboard—
I am callous to life.

No!
I'm part of the spectrum,
iota greater than eternity's whole.

Autumn

पतझड़

T. Singh

Time

Fading away in brumes of breath,

fresh rain brings memories of days
without the wrap of space.
Forged in a bang, limitless—
what has cascaded today will rise again.
A second gone, no second thoughts.

Years move—
some cold and unchanged,
some chained and warm,
some free in mist—
floating away too soon.

Autumn

October's morning canopy is azure
before fall says *adieu*.
Sugar maple blossoms yellow,
swinging tupelos black,
now rich with kingly reds and
growing mellow.

Morning dew imbues
Earth's young green sod:
the thin moist blades
rub shoulders with
fall's scattered grace.

Leaves for color wings
swirl in a crowning whirl,
now at the mercy of the Gulf winds
feeding the acorn in petite hands.

She hums as she ambles along a stream—
fall's hues preserving
her colorful ashen eyes and full womb.

Post Bloom

Tangled breathing wires,
rusted brittle spikes—
the leaves are gone,
aching without disguise.
Tethered in unsaid webs
aloof in the blue sky,
the fragile heart—pointless
to passing strangers.

They come and go,
pompous and worn,
marching
on and on.

Dice

Silence is the beat tonight—

a brewing storm,
an altered thought.
How long will this play last?

An act in the middle,
already gray from innocent jabs.
Who should think this smile is fake?

Perfected during graveyard days—
day or night, hearts already burnt.
No matter how long,

the only way to connect is to disconnect.

Halley's Comet

Silent beats—hearts lingering
in void space—
roll the dice
into a diverging pulse.

Diminishing is this
expanse of knots—
it makes us so raw
that more of us
desire less of *we*.

Dusk to dawn—
colliding gravitational waves.
Dawn to dusk—
our eccentric orbits.

We charted this bright future—
white smiles and faces gleaming
in a coma of wealth—
it mocks our dusty trail.

In full moonlight,
we bicker, quibble, fight.
On fiercely guided spheres,
we spin black holes between us.
Flesh inches away, light years apart.

It wasn't like this from the start.
I heard Halley's Comet is in flight—

a passing blip.

The orbit will signal us to hold—
eclipsed dreams can heal
once we switch off our blazing lights.

Separations

Dark clouds looming over an innocent sun
spinning around some indeterminate point
between years of upheaval and faltering love—
we are born.

My father a plumber from a plumber.
My mother, a pet store cashier.
Dad could unclog a lot of things, but the
love backed up with mutual despise was
not one of them. So
he pursued unanchored bends, and
she called in suited experts.

I met Bill from the school book club, his life
always revolving around the fine print.
His father, an expert in outer space, and
his mother, a geneticist. He now flies
coast-to-coast to keep the family tradition alive.

The infinite and microscopic lives are
stretched too thin to bind.

And my neighbor Tracy, shy and innocent Tracy,
formed untold oceans before her
mother drowned in meth waves;
Her innocent prints are threadless,
though years later,
she would marry Jason, a trooper,
an orphan of an unwarranted war.
His father was a victim of combat, and
his mother has since surrendered
to her mental state.

What is home?
Some meaningful hold
on memories;
accent walls are cold.

No one knows what happened to Coby, the
prodigy who hopped our fences from
neighboring cracked courts,
rhythms confined to restless shifts
and whistling scrimmages.
Fate spins on passing lanes.

Only on lonely mattresses,
our hearts heave.
In a vacuum,
we cling to dreams,
while our lungs learn
to leap.

  T. Singh

Dotted Line

How undeniably cold you are,
no longer the passionate shell
that solemnly kept our warmth and vows.
Your abiding words were traps;
your soulful eyes have a heartless stare.

Shut the door and follow your own damn course.
I am not a statue of stone.
You hang me loose to dry as if
I were the rag here.
You have suffocated us.
I hid your beastly scars,
but all you wanted was for me to keep a lid.
You coldly command me to spread wide,
sit tight, and serve you.

In these hollowing bursts, I am decorated dust.
Come game days, you indulge
my little garden escape.
You ruin it with food scraps,
wasted beer bottles, and listless ash.
My protests are matched by knuckled threats.

But I'm not your closet bitch here to lick,
fetch, and obey.
There is no middle path between us—
no therapy for shattered glass.
Our knot was bound with blood and burns,
but even my stitched voice is clear and loud.

On page three, sign the dotted line—
our solid line ran out of time.

Voyage

Beneath the broken plate,
a stairway curves into the unknown.
Sooner or later, everyone enters
the insipid maze.
Endless—
crimson fall,
shining summer,
      holy winters,
and blossoming spring—
all withered in interlaced arms.

A push into this darkness,
the relevant past ebbs away,
balancing fruitless.

Here, who is a raven
and who is a scavenger?

At will, the brazen darkness
consumes mirrors and memories, plundering

what the flesh and bones hide,

plundering the hours, dreams,
and smiles, plundering it all!

Darkness after all,
perfectly annihilating
      time and knots.

Red Carpet

The high heels on plush red
blow steadily away from the green.

They hold the earned slender frame,
a cheerful smile waxed with radiating fame
hazy eyes glittering in purple strikes.

There is no dearth of what's called love
or opulence bestowed—just haunting cries,
the crowd's rush, talk of the town,
an authority that seals it all.

Nothing is new to the crowded 'I'—
aloof on unscalable heights!

The world is coined and spinning,
but rattling pride comes with a price.
Vastness is venerable
colors of glory, stained,

the broken 'I' chained and—

Who will cultivate green space?

Time

is here again in its usual tide,
knocking subtly on my hardened hide.
Call it a vanilla disguise
in my burrow,
unscathed by floating allure.

Trust me, time—here again—
has turned.

I am naked in my own spotlight.

Winter

Thin Ways

When thick shades haunt
and bring breath to a halt,
go around the nurtured path;
take along the dusk and
follow the unpaved arc.

Spread crumbs for the doves.

Follow the arc.

There is always a new dawn.
When the heart brews
unspoken storms
and all that seemed together falls apart,
take a dip in the frigid pond.
Flow as love.

Broken

Look no further into my eyes—
saga of our love, unkind.
A crimson smile brings momentary cheer,
withering away in the hush of darkness.
Why carry around a lantern?
There is a *we* in *weep*,
and from the depths we hurt.
Finish the matter; carry an ax.

Loss

Night is unnecessary—these days
are dark enough, and silence is chaotic
without argument.

Moments
together are joyous, memory
is a sorrowful field

stretching beyond sky.

What unfolded on a bright day
collapsed under thunders of fate.

Cause undetermined.
Loss undying.
Breath futile.

Storm Drain

Down the storm drain
flow songs
and stains
as dream lovers
relish hours—
we had set plans.

When two beats collide,
multifaceted orbits spin.
Oh, universe lost in dreams:
what an exhaustive reel.

In flares of youth we set for stars,
build our cosmos by long shots.
In that expanding space,
delusion seeds easily.

With imprints of strain
and stains
on guilt-free hands,
curse-free lips
became deep blue recollections.

glued in red frames and
embossed with our names.

We unseal as fissures speak.

T. Singh

Dead Bond

A tug of words in my heart
battles my instinct to be free
in this hopeless fray—
the only thread
committing our knot.

Trace your steps
to the memory of our peace:
sheltered together in fortified nights,
our differences set aside.

We were good for each other then.
Now, in the barbed pain,
nothing is left
for the heart to feel
for time to keep
for memories to outlast.

No warmth, no rails, no guards—
just a friction-filled knot,
your shamelessly abusing hands
and surly tongue
lashing me at every turn.

The threat of your spiteful ammunition
keeps me a prisoner,
sentenced to endless bitterness.

Victims of Flesh

The peak glow on cheeks
fades faster than perceived.
Diminishing vantage point of age,
it hustles unnoticed on time's curves.
Victims of flesh!

Their celebration always comes to rest.

Its blind layers
are breached by hidden fears—
in fear of the lost self
or lost in itself.
Victims of flesh!

Dear ones dead or bountied.

Though,
to begin with,
holding hands is a natural thought.
Still, the bonds are washed
by the swell of knotted waves.
Victims of flesh!

Weary in the whirlpool of mistrust.

The heart's unhealed layers
uproar in sullen wilderness.
A heart needs a heart
to ignite a new warmth.
Victims of flesh!

Knitted together—an ever-diverging universe.

Wind lifts the kite

tight string
unfazed
by the
sky.

On thin spikes
held high,
paper soars
higher and
higher.

The hinge squeaks rhythmically:
hardened screws,
milled plates,
a treated wood-plank
engraved with stained glass—
a passage turns a million ways,
testament to time's
push and pull.

Listen…

The calendar silently whirls—
visible dates invisibly lost,
invisible dates visibly sought.
Within folds of print,
history and dreams forge a bond.

An oak casket crackles
and heaves, settling down
into a freshly dug trench.
The flesh will decay in silence.
Impressions on soft corners
evaporate with undue pain.

In time: bold epitaphs,
a granite plaque,
a circle of crabgrass,
a larger circle of silent arms.

Spring

Luminous

time
polished by its own path
hangs whimsically over never,
now, and ever.

Unconquerable in epics
our triumphs swell, dreams
billow, and glory rolls forth.

Undivided shining rays,
colliding days, and smiles
reveal a gathering light.

Memorable dews—
our maiden alights,
heralding faith:
the rise and fall, equitable.

Spring

Spring up, soul!
Sing with the chirping robin's chorus.

Strike the invincible mustard pose.
Reveal vibrancy in the crocus maze.

Trickle through the freeze.
Let your heart leap a beat.

Sour cherries are blossom sweet;
rejuvenated hydrangeas, green.

Ghostly buds sprout to
gushing streams.

Pluck the infinite abloom—
it's Spring.

T. Singh

Orange Cleaner

endless wash cycles
a full closet in an empty house
a familiar glimpse of the vanished vase
new stains on the runner

the orange cleaner, lost

what burden to carry
when loss is visible
what further words to say
when remembering what is lost—
in an instant, gone

a cherished knot
once anchored, holding soft
careful steps

a queen bed without the queen—

and the king, a frenzied bumblebee
following an ethereal scent

April

She has a bold heart,
youthful skin, and piercing eyes—
a beautiful spine sucked hollow
by unmarked strides.

In shadows of leaves on paved streets
at the corner, she holds thick ink-fated
lines. Sharpie words confine
the flowery smile
an invisible weight.
Is there an untouched bloom?

Walking the steps, a voice careens me,
the beat shrinking on cardboard.
A spirit consumes the backdrop:
a ripening memory,
a deafening block.
How many ticks does a season last?
Is it all accounted for in wants?

I'm hesitant to ask, and her eyes say a lot
with haste; she puts away weary nights
but then spills about days:
"Rocky, my dog, was intentionally poisoned.
My partner gave me a black eye."
Unwritten rules are the broken ways
violence breathes the orphaned void.
To keep the ushering darkness at bay,
she colors her hair in vibrant hues.
Is there a color bright enough
to pull apart dark?

T. Singh

She is there, crosses legs, silent, in the crossways
of the silenced. There with lavender streaks
and scalded palm lines, a half-smile
receding gum line.

Crisp leaves curl on our scattered signs.
Inscribed somewhere—
April is abloom.

Powder and Pain

Just one stray bullet destroyed it all.
Father, pierced by cold brass—
a hole in his broad chest
crushed their budding lives.
Mother slid down, down the pint drain,
and the son adopted a heartless street.

On curbs, he kept his brazen mold,
built a ring that ran alleys
and silenced doors.
Friends like hollowing termites
left only foes to lean on and revere.
Surrounded by dusty moles,
brass knuckles hold his fort.
Cloak and clock on trigger,
he lives pierced with fear.

Little James christened.
King James of powder and pain.

There is nothing subtle about his ways:
his chest, scarred,
his labored breath pushes tight
against the tinted space.
He tracks these years on withering arms—
on blocks, his dope is more liberating
than holy mass.

Dead knots are time's prey.
Sprinkling powder, sprinkling holy water—
to him it makes no difference.

T. Singh

War Zone

On an unmanned moonless night,
I ran into some young soldiers
at a bar, locally known as the ballistic flesh bazaar.
The troops were out for the night, looking
to sugarcoat their pulsating fears.
Virgin to the vibes of war, they
awaited the last call.

Beyond the flickering neon sign,
and the loosely guarded door,
the bar was a deceptive den bustling with warm bodies
in vogue with corrosive circles of smoke
playing forth their own rhythms of mortality.

The dance floor was a minefield—
sweet booby traps, marching boots at ease,
swirling with edgy chicks who tapped on high heels.
Their lust for breath, flesh, and action
flared high in cocktails.

Breasts brushed against broad chests.
Their adrenaline was in peak rush,
the blaze of night entrenched
in warm arms.
In the eager dawn,
an army of cold arms will leap
into a deafening dance.

An unfolding and reverberating night—
will tomorrow's fortress draw new blood?
Which hue? Moments burn—
breath absorbs the searing incense.
In whose honor does the dust elevate these hollow holds?

Foot soldiers in ambush with fate—
Bleeding sway, wounded say.

T. Singh

Candle

All unknowns for a flickering flame
visible, thin, and diminishing in wax age.

Fires to kindle
Desires to burn

Elixir pulverizes accumulated soot;
fuel brightens the eternal muse.

Wisdom to sink
Quests to elevate

All mysteries for a wick
are lifeless in a shallow pit.

Rosary to scale
Burden to relinquish

Tears soften our ego's stance;
smiles nourish our hours.

Victories to slay
Losses to resurrect

Despite burning, the hardened heart
learns to kneel.
All mysteries are for the molten wax
that burns for moment's peace.

Glow

When one works with soil,
an earthly scent overwhelms life's sweat.

Stubborn clay fizzles,
spinning an endless garden to tend.

Acts of gardening:

Kneeling
      knock on the hours to root
Weeding
      reminder for the remainder to uproot
Amending
      balance to seek
Tilling
      momentum to keep
Sowing
      tap onto continuum
Irrigating
      stream of acceptance
Harvesting
      bliss beyond season

When the final almanac turns,
soiled hands are fired in an immortal kiln,
      a hue that glows then blossoms forth.

T. Singh

Void

मूंठ

T. Singh

Reflective

Impetuous holds—
desires flare and soar,
memories cipher.
Our vacancy
hums for an aerie.

Edgeless and incisive
with a keen spear,
we dangle frictionless
on feathers and fear.

Resonating in silence,
our unrest searches
for a name. Wings beg
for space, and our flight
becomes a cult.

Void

Void is deprived of complexity,
color, and monotone blending.

Far and near, near and far,
all condenses into no form.

No Nashville bloom,
no Mississippi guilt,
no pole star to align.

Perfectly hollow,
      swallows perfectly.

Liberate

Walls of thoughts
of unjust walls.

Pearls coated in perils
perils contained in pearls.

Bare necks adorned
with emeralds that invite
sharp edges to bare necks.

Squeezing alleys push out
warm breath that squeezes
alleys of unforgiving roar.

A white swan is
dark circles biting dust.

A black swan is
a halo liberating
manned darkness.

Sojourn

Here and there on the sidewalk,
trimming the grass in repetitive motions,
humming a melody while playing guitar,
our journeys feel trapped under glass jars.

Our cherished milestones float away,
and a playbook of earn and burn
fuels our frenzied craze.

Trading chubby innocence for wrinkled arrogance
our sandcastles abandoned in lieu of glass palaces.
The might we serve is a trap,
heart-tucked and *me first*.

Secluded now, we draw comfort in distance—
footprints murky,
smiles deaf,
beats sighless,
breath pulseless.

Suffocated, pause eluded—
caustic fears,
stale dreams,
numb moments.

Our sojourns are scant displays.

T. Singh

What checks does a five-eye ivy need?

It grows selfishly
along high ridges or fertile plains,
vile and pervasive.
Young guns or old barrels,

callous cowboys or delicate darlings—
it grips with a potent choke.
Ivy's sprouted seeds
nourished by warm thoughts—
they know how to haunt!

Feeble minds and maverick hearts
are subtly ruled by this poisonous czar.
In the lopsided battle,
we wax armored warriors.

Five-eye ivy crushes with precise spite.
Will honor ever come this way?

Suspended Rails

Will the Pacific carry salt for old wounds
in its hum?

We churn the hours like fresh prints
on coarse sand. As a kid, I walked the suspended paths

left hand fingers running on the rail
right hand firm in father's soft palm.

His hands resonate on a different plane, sure and
gasping to break away from this suspended space.

No reasons, no falsework, just the urge
to catch tomorrow. Left tender fingers dangle forever.

Suspended between time's crest and trough,
I hold fast to the moment.

In the maze of runaway tides,
the rail of time's suspension evolved into an anchor hold.

Untimely rip currents swept away high friends.
Mother fell, a delusional shell in eddies, lost in dates.

Suspended above a sea of loose grips, those defining years
were sheer tests.

Now the little fingers clasp them, a girl to her father,
her love and trust in seasoned grip. The twisted cables

hold tight to the rails; the rusted bits are often brushed
with fresh memory paint.

T. Singh

Muse

Shades of gray and crimson
play above a depth of blue.
One mind and heart—one spirit—
crisscross endless thoughts.
Wants and songs, sin and sane,
ceaselessly collide.

When dark night-waves pull in,
I learn: alone
we all whirl in the same
dusk and dawn.

Bliss

How does emptiness swallow
when there is nothing to feed?

There is no absence of need.
Why is fulfillment shallow?

Low-lying desires sprout an inferno
while deep in us is an ocean of calm.

What makes thinking
think it will dig itself from
yesterday's webs,
buzzing now, and anxious horizons?

No matter the free path
the fragile breath clings on,
it's always on a ledge.

In our voided hustles,
bliss remains undiscovered

T. Singh

Time

ticks faster than exhales of breath.
From one undone to another,
life unfolds.

why does time have needles

Paced for reason
within measurable tides,
long arms divide seeded drives,
short legs with memorable depth
a consistent tick.

The bang stays afloat
from pod to plant and plant to pod.

The unwary undone leashes what's done.

Welcome

These are my looks:
sculpted clay
annotated on a borrowed mask.
Crisp cheeks spin on a karmic wheel.
Diluted whiskers stretched on a clock.
Flowing beard cornered by fate.
Straws of cosmetic honor—
boasting in the head,
splashing on the nose,
breeding in the lungs,
glaring on the blades,
blaring on the tongue.

Welcome to my depthless slate.

The essence of flow:
cornered in my heart's bubbling chambers,
contemplating blossom, while cozy in tangles.
Though the unsolicited pangs ceaselessly knock,
the reckoning thud finds solace in cyclical feats.

Welcome to my desolate state.

T. Singh

Consciously aware that the moment
of dawn is pitched beyond illusive arcs:
still the poet, Singh is devoted to false charms.
What began as a true thread is now a false web.
What began as a blissful exhale is a burgeoning chain.
The vehicle to liberate is an exhausted slave.

Welcome to my captive fate.

Near and far, all evaporate.
Reflected prints vanish.
Imprints hollow for eternity are satiated by a glance.
What has been stagnant for eons could
flow with a grace.

Welcome to my mortal-immortal stay.

T. Singh

Acknowledgement

Grateful for the hours, the bonds,
and the blooming ink.

Grateful for the pause, the heritage,
the stage and the blank page.

Grateful for the warm hearts, the knocks,
trusting holds and knotted space.

Grateful for the sketch, the silhouette,
flesh, and the emancipating soul

Grateful for the nest, the quest,
breath and the undying words!

T. Singh

A Poet

is an opus of rising crests
and plunging troughs,
nodes anchoring our chain-links.

In the wave of his craft
our pulse and knots ride

beyond residue and decree
of the currents, a flag bearer of revolt.

When darkness runs roil,
his pen dismantles the illusion
and his ink an illuminance.

Within his churn,
the chapters unfold:
poet, a keeper.

Taran Singh is a poet and photographer.
Born & raised in the Himalayas,
he currently resides in the bay area,
California.

T. Singh

Time & Knots
Taran Singh

Cover Illustration & Concept · Renata Cuellar

Cover Designers · Patrícia Oliveira, Ryane Aclain, Kayla Elizabeth Jaeb

Book Designer · Patrícia Oliveira

Gurmukhi Calligraphy · Kamaljeet Kaur

Gurmukhi Consultant · Gurmeet Kaur

Senior Editor · Hannah Warren

Poetry Editors · Hannah Warren, Nia Howard, Cassandra Rockwood-Rice

Consulting Editors · Jeszika Art, Harminder Kaur, Laura Bernell, Lisa Favicchia

Marketing Lead · Alana Zamora

Illustrators · Lauma Sliŋķe, Olivia Reed, Lea Zalinskis, Ryane Aclain, Renata Cuellar

Website · www.timeandknots.com

Email · timeandknots@gmail.com

Instagram · @timeandknots

21867996R00049

Made in the USA
San Bernardino, CA
06 January 2019